IMAGES
of Scotland

HAMILTON AND BLANTYRE

The manager and his staff line up outside Hamilton Central Co-operative Society's No. 3 Branch in Low Waters Road at Hutchison Street. It is 1938 and Burnbank and Blantyre had their own Co-ops. The Hamilton Co-op was founded in 1879 and amalgamated with the independent Chapel Street Society in 1903. The headquarters were in Gateside Street and on the stretch between Avon Street and Woodside Walk you could get all you might need in life's journey, from the cradle to the funeral parlour, round the corner in Quarry Street. That last is all that remains, now run by the CWS. Like many others, including Burnbank and Blantyre, the Hamilton Society failed to meet the challenge of modern retailing. In 1938, though, almost every family had their Co. number, and many can quote it to this day. It is Shopping Week, Thursday 7 to 16 April, leading up to Easter. There's a Mannequin Parade in the town hall and a 'cheery intimation' tells you that the divi is a welcome two shillings in the pound. Many mostly forgotten brands on display include 'Bluebell Margarine, 'Co Sauce", 'Unitas" breakfast foods, 'Lutona Cocoa" and a selection of other SCWS products from Shieldhall, the vast Co-op industrial park in Glasgow's south side.

Cover Illustration: Peacock Cross on the occasion of the Royal Visit, July 1953 (see pp. 92-93).

IMAGES of Scotland

HAMILTON AND BLANTYRE

Compiled by
Peter Stewart

TEMPUS

First published 1999
Copyright © Peter Stewart, 1999

Tempus Publishing Limited
The Mill, Brimscombe Port,
Stroud, Gloucestershire, GL5 2QG

ISBN 0 7524 1613 8

Typesetting and origination by
Tempus Publishing Limited
Printed in Great Britain by
Midway Clark Printing, Wiltshire

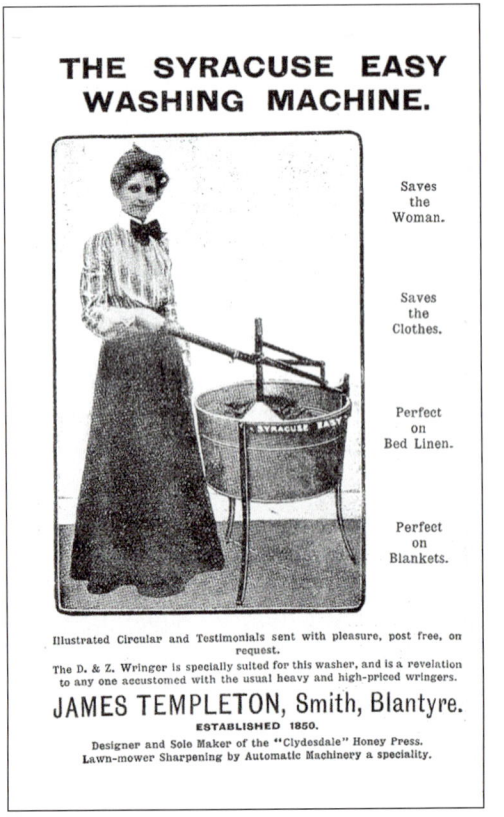

Advertisment from *How to Nurse the Patient*, published by Blantyre Nursing Association, 1908.

Contents

Introduction		7
1.	Old Cross, New Cross	9
2.	The Old Town and Palace	23
3.	Cadzow Street	37
4.	Almada Street and Bothwell Road	51
5.	New Cross to Low Waters	61
6.	The Outskirts	73
7.	Burnbank	91
8.	Blantyre	109

Hamilton, between the two World Wars, from an aerial photgraph taken in 1928. The Clyde is at the top of the picture. Tuphall Road (A) is shown from its junction with Quarry Street and Bent Road, with the gasholder (B) to its right. The back of Johnstone Street tenements (C) has Woodside School beyond. Selkirk Street (D) ran through from Portland Place (E) to cross Tuphall Road. Scott Street (F) and Butterburn Park Street (G) climb, uninterrupted, from Tuphall Road and across Burnblea Street (H). Low Patrick Street (J) has the old Hippodrome at its foot. Central Station (K) and the former Town Hall are on the left of the picture. Before many years had passed the fields at the bottom of the picture would be built on as the council housing programme got under way. (PPC, published by Valentine, 204092)

Introduction

Hamilton is a town not short of history. When, a few years before the battle of Bannockburn, Sir Gilbert of Hamilcombe, grandson of the Earl of Leicester, rashly praised Robert the Bruce, 'one John de Spencer gave him a blow, which arrogant treatment he resented so highly, that encountering him the next day, he killed him; and to avoid punishment fled to Scotland, where he was well received by King Robert: who to make amends for what he had forfaulted on his account at home, generously rewarded him with the Barony of Cadzow, in the County of Lanark, then an appendage of the Crown.' The three cinquefoils on the town's Crest relate to the Leicester connection.

Cadzow (or Cadyou) was the ancient name for the district in which the medieval town grew by the banks of the Clyde. High above a wooded gorge on the Avon cling the ruins of Cadzow Castle, 800 or more years old. In the troubled times of Queen Mary it was besieged more than once by her foes and finally taken apart in 1579.

Other romantic legends date from long before the time the Hamiltons came riding into town. Rederech, King of Strathclyde, had as wife and queen, Langoreth, who lost her ring carrying on with a lusty knight. St Mungo came to the rescue and the ring was miraculously found inside a fish caught where the Avon meets the Clyde. All this happened in the sixth century. The Royals, thereafter, were converted to Christianity – a good tale and the origin of the fish and the ring in Glasgow's Crest.

Hamilton's status has often changed. A Burgh of Barony from 1456, the town became a Royal Burgh in Queen Mary's reign. In 1670, in the days of the formidable Duchess Anne, it was downgraded to a Burgh of Regality and royal status was never restored, though not for the want of trying. The Reform Act of 1832 made the town a Parliamentary Burgh. Hamilton ceased being a Burgh in 1975 and became the centre of a larger Hamilton District in Strathclyde Region. In 1996 the region's short life ended and Hamilton is now the administrative centre of South Lanarkshire.

The town no longer hugs the Clyde so closely. The ancient parish church and the houses round about gave way to the Duke's rebuilt palace in the eighteenth century, and what was later called the Old Town was built on the higher ground outside the palace walls. The Duke built a splendid new parish church, designed by William Adam, and a bridge over the Cadzow Burn that carries Cadzow Street across it was built by a later duke in the nineteenth century. The palace, alas, disappeared in the 1920s for the sake of coal. Lennoxlove, in the east, later became the official residence of the Dukes of Hamilton.

Weaving was a thriving home industry and some single-storey weavers' cottages, modernised into *bijou* homes, can still be seen. The town was also well known for lacemaking. Hamilton was a staging post on the route to England and the Old Head Inn, now the town's Museum, was on the Duke's estate. It was long a garrison town but only the Cameronians Museum and the name Barrack Street remind us of that. From the mid-nineteenth century, for a hundred years, coal dominated the district.

Population rocketed from 9,620 in the 1851 census, 24,863 in 1891 to over 40,000 before boundary changes made comparisons difficult. For all that, it remained a compact town until the new estates, from the 1920s onward, spread out into the fields. By 1878 Burnbank and Low Waters had become part of the Burgh and the miners' rows multiplied in these parts and beyond. Though the pits closed after the Second World War, the cramped and unhealthy dwellings lingered on for many years.

From the late fifties the Town Council's liberal policy on private housing development, together with continued council building, changed the face of the Burgh and brought in newcomers from all over. Ridding Hamilton of its own slums and taking some of Glasgow's overspill saw new estates built in a wide arc from Whitehill and Hillhouse to Eddlewood. Only two, fairly modest, tower blocks went up and sensible tenancy policies prevented these being vandalised, though they proved expensive to maintain. Many council houses have since been bought by their tenants.

Loss of population from miners moving east to new pits in Fife and Clackmannan, or families on emigrant fares to Australia or off to find work in Canada, was made good by newcomers attracted by the houses built for sale by Weir, Wimpey and other developers. Many came from Glasgow at a time when private house building there was not encouraged and commuting from a home 'on the edge of the countryside' was an attractive option. A significant number of new Hamiltonians from other parts of Britain as well as from the Commonwealth helped to produce a more cosmopolitan mix. With these changes has come an explosion of restaurants and other outlets to satisfy all thirsts and appetites, attracting patrons from many parts.

Hamilton, like all the old mining and industrial towns, is now a cleaner and healthier place. Though not all would agree with some of the 'improvements', few mourn the Victorian slums or the once depressing lifestyle in estates such as Burnbank's 'Jungle' and 'Sing-Sing', or 'Wine Valley', where so many decent families enjoyed so few amenities and suffered years of abuse. The present on-going plans for the centre are ambitious and imaginative. Hamilton is not alone in its loss of so much local industry, but it continues to attract newcomers to the business parks and industrial estates in and around. White-collar jobs and supermarkets may lack the comradeship of 'real work' or the cosiness of corner shops, but it is hard to swim against the tide.

Burnbank and Blantyre share a common boundary and each has its separate identity which is explored in the introduction to its own Section (pp. 91 & 109 respectively.)

This collection of photographs aims to show things and people as they were. It is not possible to include everything or everybody, but perhaps it will stir memories in some and for those too young to recall any of the sights and fashions of those days it may give an insight into how things were in times past.

Acknowledgements

I have had help from many people in putting together this collection of photographs and owe thanks for information and reminiscences enthusiastically offered. For their help and co-operation I am grateful to the staff of the Community Resources Department of South Lanarkshire Council, including Linda Barrett and Joyce Brown; Norman Reid and Cilla Jackson of the University of St Andrews Library, where the James Valentine & Sons postcard archive is held, and Mr Duncan White of Whiteholme (Publishers) Ltd. Individual items are acknowledged with thanks in the text. My thanks are due also to His Grace the Duke of Hamilton, Alexander Cunningham, Jim Hamilton, Brian Lynas, Walter McGowan, Robert McLeod, Gordon Mitchell, Robert Smellie, Sandy Smellie, Myra Syme, David Thompson and William Wallace. The staff in the Hamilton Library have been very helpful. David Buxton, Senior Editor and Matthew Forlow and Campbell McCutcheon of Tempus Publishing have offered valuable help and support. My wife, Margaret, has helped as before in checking the text and offering advice.

Abbreviations

PPC - Picture Post Card
Valentine - image reproduced by kind permission of St Andrews University Library from a postcard published by James Valentine & Sons, Dundee, in my own collection unless otherwise noted.

One
Old Cross, New Cross

The Old Cross and the New Cross, connected by the lower part of Quarry Street, are best known to all as the Bottom Cross and the Top Cross. The 'Old Cross' is not, in fact, a piece of ancient history, for the town centre only moved from the Tolbooth when the Duke did his rebuilding. The present road layout results from the need in 1903 to give the new tram service from Motherwell a curve into the town less tight than that allowed by entry into Cadzow Street from Castle Street. Quarry Street was the old path to Donaghdee Quarry and is still Hamilton's main street for the smaller shops, though few of the older local businesses remain. The buildings are mostly nearing entry into their second century, looking handsome since they were cleaned. The street was part pedestrianised in the 1970s and all has changed once again, with Quarry Street reinvented while Castle Street now leads into the new Town Square and on to a modern shopping paradise and sports park. Never again shall we see the caravans of the travelling fair in the Low Parks at Easter and the September weekend. The ancient Townhead Street and Duke Street connected the two Crosses with Carlisle Road, and until the Regent Way shopping centre happened in the sixties there was a chaotic, higgledy-piggledy area between them of old businesses, tenements and smaller dwellings. Street names redolent of the past, such as Baillies Causeway disappeared forever. This had been the route taken by Bailie Mather and Bailie Patrick, whose name survives in High and Low Patrick Street, to meetings in the Tolbooth nearly 200 years ago. The New Cross proper, dates from around 1843 and here the Town Hall was built in 1863. It ended its life, minus its leaning tower, in 1963, as a police station. The department store built on the site is one of the few modern buildings in Quarry Street, which is now graced with sculpture, plinths and carved messages on some of the paving. The street continues uphill past the Cross.

Quarry Street from the Old Cross to the New, *c*.1930. Montague Burton's shop, built in 1927, used stone from the palace. Earlier, the street narrowed here into 'the neck of the bottle.' All these buildings survive. Above the White Horse Bar are the newsagent ('What to Back at Newmarket Today') and G. Fraioli's 'Continental Restaurant.' On the left, halfway up, is Regent Street, replaced by Regent Way in the 1960s. In the distance is the Town Hall tower. (PPC, W. Holmes & Co., Herald Series)

The Old Cross in 1929. The buses, which would seal the fate of the trams, wait at the crossing. Douglas Chambers, housing the Douglas & Clydesdale Bar, matches a red sandstone building on the opposite side of Castle Street. Keith Street leads to La Scala Cinema, empty today after a spell as a bingo hall. (PPC, Valentine, 205993)

The Old Cross. By 1933 the trams have gone. A busy afternoon and a crowd of neatly dressed, flat capped men wait on the kerb. There always seemed to be men in their 'bunnets' at street corners. Below, it is 1963 and not a lot has changed. G. Fraioli's 'Continental Restaurant' is now the 'Cafe Grill.' Harrison, the tailor is still around today. At the bus stop is Cooper's Supermarket. An old chain, famous for their tea and coffee, its Hamilton shop was long in Cadzow Street. It became 'Fine Fare' and then a clothing store. 'No Waiting' but no yellow lines yet. (PPCs, Valentine 219534, D8108)

Townhead Street at the Old Cross. Tram No. 25 is bound for Larkhall, a service which ran from 1905 to 1928. This is an Edwardian view, but the buildings are little changed today. (PPC, Hartmann 4313.9)

Townhead Street, about the turn of the century. The hotel remembered by many as the Commercial, but now the Hamilton Town is on the left. Opposite, all has changed and the street has recently become a cul-de-sac. (PPC, 'Red Star Series')

12

Quarry Street, 1938, at the entrance to Regent Street, on the right The Fifty Shilling Tailor has arrived and True-Form shoes replace Stewart's, while S.E. Becket was a jeweller. Sharp's (est. 1865) Photographic Studio is still there today and Fraioli's Ice Cream is promoted on their gable end. (PPC, Valentine A6837)

The 'neck of the bottle' at the foot of the street. Cinnamond, outfitters there, were famed for their advertising – 'Ho! Ho!! Ho!!! Who was it clothed you when a boy? Made Mother's heart rebound with joy? As she clasped her darling boy? CINNAMOND!' Quarry Place, left, once 'Herrin' Square' from the fishwives' presence, ended in a pend which led to Chapel Street. William Glass, fruiterer was at the corner until moving into the redeveloped Place in the 1970s. (PPC, Cynicus Publishing Co., 1904)

The street was a main traffic route but only an Austin Cambridge, Chivers van and Central SMT bus are here on a quiet day. Skelton's pub is at the Cross and the fashion revolution was in the future – not an anorak in sight, no jeans and not one pair of trainers. The mini-skirt is still light years away. (PPC, Valentine, D1610, 1956)

Regent Street, now Regent Way. The house has become an Alliance & Leicester branch, with the original doorway but with bow windows at street level. Regent Street did not take its name directly from George III's heir, but from the Regent Bar at the Quarry Street corner when the street was laid out in 1887. (photograph by courtesy of Myra Syme)

It is 1950 and the Wolseley's AVA 1 plates would sell well today. 'V', 'VA' and 'VD' registrations were Lanarkshire's, with 'V0' one of the few zeros in existence. On the right, Sam Pollock, licensed grocer was well known in the town. On the other side of the street, the 'Waverley' (Stop Here for Good Beer') is long gone, as have Agnew the fishmonger, Ross's dairies (a big Glasgow chain) and Jean Frame's tearoom. (PPC, Valentine, B3284)

Waddiefield, 12 Baillies Causeway, a Victorian villa, was another casualty of the shopping mall development. Opposite was a red sandstone tenement, Allan Place. The street connected Regent Street with Duke Street at its six-way junction with Miller Street. In the background can be seen Di Mambro's ice cream factory. (Photograph by kind permission of Myra Syme)

Di Mambro's ice cream factory in Holmes Street, which connected Duke Street, opposite St John's church, with Baillies Causeway. (Photograph by kind permission of Myra Syme)

Alexander Archibald & Son, at 9 Holmes Street, dealt in high-class furniture, built to last. Holmes Street branched off Duke Street at an angle, near the New Cross, to join Baillies Causeway. When the street was demolished, Archibald's moved to the top floor of an ancient, crumbling doss house in Church Street which, not before time, went out of business. (Photograph by kind permission of Myra Syme)

Looking to the town hall and New Cross about 1930. A car is moving from Duke Street to Brandon Street and behind it is the LMS Central Station. Shops on the left include the Buttercup Dairy and Woolworth's. 'Invalid Port' is on sale on the right and the pawnbroker's three brass balls are beyond.

Woolworth's in Quarry Street, a few shops down from the Town Hall, was an L-shaped store, with the other entrance in Duke Street. It moved to the new shopping mall in 1968. The building survives but not Bannatyne & Jackson, nurserymen, Robert Baxter the butcher or Alex Falconer the jeweller. (Photograph by kind permission of Myra Syme)

The Town Hall, seen here around 1914, was built in 1861 and demolished in 1963. The steeple began to lean over Duke Street on the right of the photograph, and was taken down in the 1950s. At the time this view was taken it was losing its main function, as the new building in Cadzow Street was nearly ready. (PPC, Davidson & Sons, Kirkcaldy)

The New Cross in 1950. The road surface is still whinstone setts and the Town Hall still has its tower. Excelsior Stores & Travel Agency was a long-established local firm which survived until the 1980s but the balustraded front shop is now a bank after a few years as a National Coal Board (remember it?) showroom. (PPC, Valentine B3285)

A year later and the Town Hall is truncated. Duke Street to the top of Holmes Street is beyond. The British Linen Bank merged with the Bank of Scotland. A Bentley, GUS 4, crosses to Brandon Street, but there is little else moving. A Celtic FC Supporters Club are advertising a dance at the Town Hall in Cadzow Street. (PPC, Valentine B4395)

New Cross from the 'new' Duke Street, 1970s. Baird's department store replaces the Town Hall and as far as St John's church (off the picture, behind the tree) all else made way for the five traffic lanes, Marks & Spencer and a car park. Quarry Street (right) was still open to one-way traffic. The building at the corner of Lamb Street (centre right) would soon be replaced by the New Cross Centre, housing the Fine Fare (now Somerfield) store. (PPC, Whitehome (Publishers) Ltd, Dundee, 4329W)

Townhead Street in the 1960s when Blackswell Lane, between the Argyll & Sutherland Bar and the ABC Cinema was just that, a narrow lane. Now it is to be the route for all traffic in and out of the town centre from Motherwell Road and the roundabouts. The Trocadero Dance Hall had the Roxy Cinema beside it, before that became a nightclub, opened by the film star Broderick Crawford. The ABC, now derelict, is due to suffer the same fate as the Troc. and the Roxy, both gone.(Photograph by kind permission of Myra Syme)

Tenements on Low Patrick Street, when it was just a narrow way up to Duke Street. (Photograph by kind permission of Myra Syme)

Blackswell Lane, left, meets Townhead Street and the impressive illuminated display for Skelton's Argyll & Sutherland Bar, taken down when Blackswell Lane was widened and Keith Street became one-way. The Odeon, with its three screens, closd in September 1999, to be replaced by a multiplex, somewhere, sometime. The houses beyond are where KwikFit later was, and is no more. Townhead Street is now closed at Blackswell Lane. (Photograph by kind permission of Myra Syme)

The Hippodrome Music Hall, at the bottom of Low Patrick Street, opened in 1907, owned by E.H.Bostock, who also had the Zoo and Circus in Glasgow and ran the Victoria Music Hall in Quarry Street. It burnt down in 1946 and for some years market stalls occupied the site on Saturdays. (Photograph reproduced by kind permission of South Lanarkshire District Council)

One
The Old Town and the Palace

The triangle bounded by Cadzow Street, Castle Street and Muir Street is still known as the Old Town. The oldest building, now the Hamilton Museum, was once a posting inn built in 1696, and was a house for David Crawford, Duchess Anne's secretary. Much of the rest of the Old Town is now council-built dwellings from the 1920s which replaced the eighteenth century 'Hieton', itself a result of the third Duke's plan to shift the medieval township of Hamilton and give him space to rebuild and improve the Palace. His wife Anne had succeeded as Duchess in her own right when her uncle, the 2nd Duke, died of his wounds after the Battle of Worcester. The Palace was a place of staggering magnificence, a fitting seat for the premier duke of Scotland, filled with treasures of untold worth. Duchess Anne (1632-1716) 'a lady, who for constancy of Mind, evenness of Temper, solidity of Judgment, and an unaffected Piety, will leave a shining Character, as well as an example to Posterity, for her Conduct as a Wife, a Mother, a Mistress and in all other Conditions of Life,' was one of those formidable women who through the ages managed to overcome the contemporary handicap of being female to leave their mark on history. The Duke's political ambitions in those turbulent days often kept him in Edinburgh. Their sympathies in the 'killing times' were strong enough for the Palace to be a refuge for Covenanters seeking protection. She was succeeded by her son James, the 4th Duke, who preferred Edinburgh to Hamilton and liked London much more than either. In 1712, after despatching Lord Mohun in a Hyde Park duel with one shot, he died of his own wounds. Before the end of the nineteenth century the extravagance of Alexander, the 10th Duke, known to the townspeople as 'El Magnifico', was starting to be felt, and a sale of art treasures at Christies in 1882 raised the then huge sum of almost £400,000. The family were already using Dungavel Lodge, beyond Strathaven, as their residence in the area before the Palace was pulled down in the 1920s for the coal beneath – its fading splendour is remembered by some of the oldest townspeople. The Ducal family fortunes had never recovered from the building of the Mausoleum, which happily survives in the care of the Council. The anachronistic street names largely survived: Postgate, Grammar School Square, Sheilinghill and many others. The Castle Street and Muir Street of recent days are unrecognisable, the former now a path to the new town square, the latter rebuilt to cope with the increased traffic. Between the two streets a web of dual carriageways and roundabouts has lately grown. Hamilton's boundary extends to the Clyde and Strathclyde Park and along Motherwell Road to the bridge which connects the two towns.

The Old Cross on a Fair Day in the 1880s, with market stalls in Castle Street and no end of customers. William Wallace, the undertaker, in the Douglas & Clydesdale Hotel building, later moved to the New Cross and finally came to rest lower down Castle Street past Postgate. This building and that at the opposite corner were taken down when Keith Street was opened.

Above and left: The Tolbooth (the Old Jail) in Castle Street at the bottom of Muir Street was built in 1643 and taken down a few years after the Second World War, by which time it was unsafe due to subsidence and dry rot. On the balcony, prisoners were shown to the abusive public. The barred doorway below it marks the top of an outside stair, removed by Duchess Anne. It was later used as a pillory. Life inside was not always without its comforts; visitors were allowed to bring food and drink and merry parties were held, with the compliance of the poorly paid jailers. However, for some it was a short last walk to Gallowshill. In these photographs by the late Robert McLeod in the 1920s, the forbidding wall round the Palace Grounds is seen curling into Muir Street at Hamilton's 'Devil's Elbow.'(Photographs reproduced by kind permission of Robert McLeod Jnr)

New Wynd from Grammar School Square to the Tolbooth. The eighteenth century homes, with their crow-step gables, were replaced in the late 1920s and the street was closed up. At its foot was the site of the original Old Cross. (PPC, 'Wrench Series', c.1908)

The Old Town, or Hieton, from the Cadzow Street bridge. The Green had a communal drying area and, with the Cadzow Burn running through, is now a well-kept park with a newly created pathway under Cadzow Street and along the wooded burn. No washing hanging out these days, though. The Palace in the background is flying the flag. (PPC, 'Brandon Series', c.1904, Stuart Marshall Collection)

'Sir' John Williamson, one of the town's well-known characters, was a figure of fun, sometimes cruel. 'Jock o' the Law' was a hawker from Kilbarchan. He was deluded that he was a knight and rode a horse at the celebrations in Glasgow for King Edward's visit after the Coronation, but was unseated when boys pricked his horse. He died in Hartwood Hospital in 1910. (PPC, 'Brandon Series', c.1902)

The Brandon Series.

"Sir" John Williamson.
From an photo by Constable Jenkins, Lanarkshire Constabulary.

The Brandon Series,

THOMAS WALLS.
A Handyman of Hamilton. He is of Irish extraction, but was born in the North of England. Locally he is called "Tommy, the Rat," and rather prides himself in the belief that he can rid the country of rodents.

Thomas Walls, described as a 'Handyman of Hamilton', was born in the North of England of Irish extraction and was a familiar figure in the town around the turn of the century. Known as 'Tommy the Rat' from his pride in his rat catching ability, he is seen on this Brandon Series postcard sitting astride a child's model horse in a studio. (PPC, c.1902)

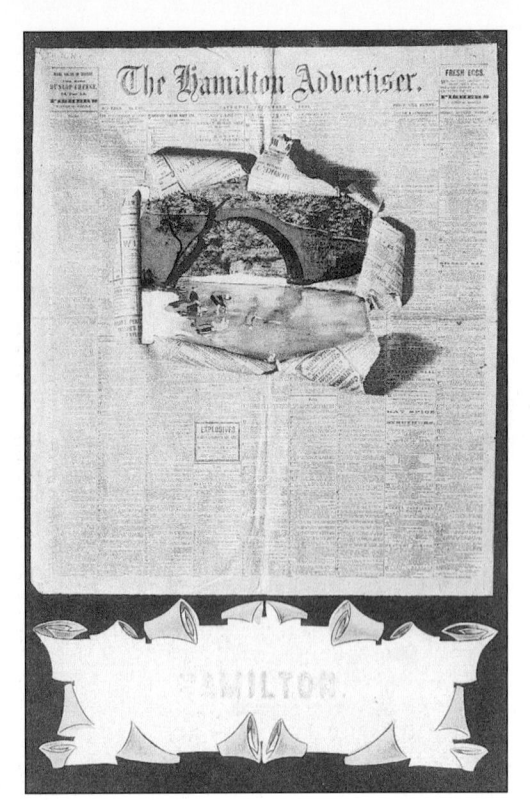

The Hamilton Advertiser was in its 51st year when this issue appeared on September 8, 1906. It is still going strong, published from Campbell Street in the Old Town. The bridge (inset) is the 'Roman Bridge', over the River Calder, now a feature on the far shore of Strathclyde Park. Although the bridge is not itself thought to date from Roman times, the remains of a Roman bath house were uncovered nearby in the 1970s when the park was being laid out. (PPC, W. Hill & Co. Ltd.)

The north front of the Palace, rebuilt in 1819. The grand Portico's double row of Corinthian columns, each fashioned from a single block of stone, was hauled from the quarry at Dalserf by a team of thirty horses. In the magnificently ornate interior was a notable black marble staircase, which during the demolition was carefully packed and stored in a builder's yard. It is said that it was later sold for £34. Many households in Hamilton have items said to have 'come frae the Palace.'

After the Palace was taken down, the land passed to the Burgh for recreation and here, in the Low Parks, Douglas, the 14th Duke, is wearing his RAF Squadron tie, and is standing beside Mr Alex Smellie, President at the County Agricultural Show in the 1950s. In 1933 the then Marquis of Douglas & Clydesdale piloted the first plane to fly over Everest. Air Commodore during the Second World War, he was a flying instructor, as were his three brothers, Nigel, Malcolm and David, the last two losing their lives while on service. In 1941 an unwelcome visitor, Rudolf Hess, who claimed to have met the Duke at an air show, dropped in near Eaglesham, missing Dungavel by several miles, and was promptly arrested. The 14th Duke died in 1973, being succeeded by his son, the present holder of the title, Angus, 15th Duke. (Photograph by kind permission of Robert Smellie)

The front and rear aspects of the Palace, from Edwardian postcard views. (Above: published by W.Ritchie & Sons, Edinburgh. Below: published by Marcus Wane & Co., Edinburgh; K.Norris Collection)

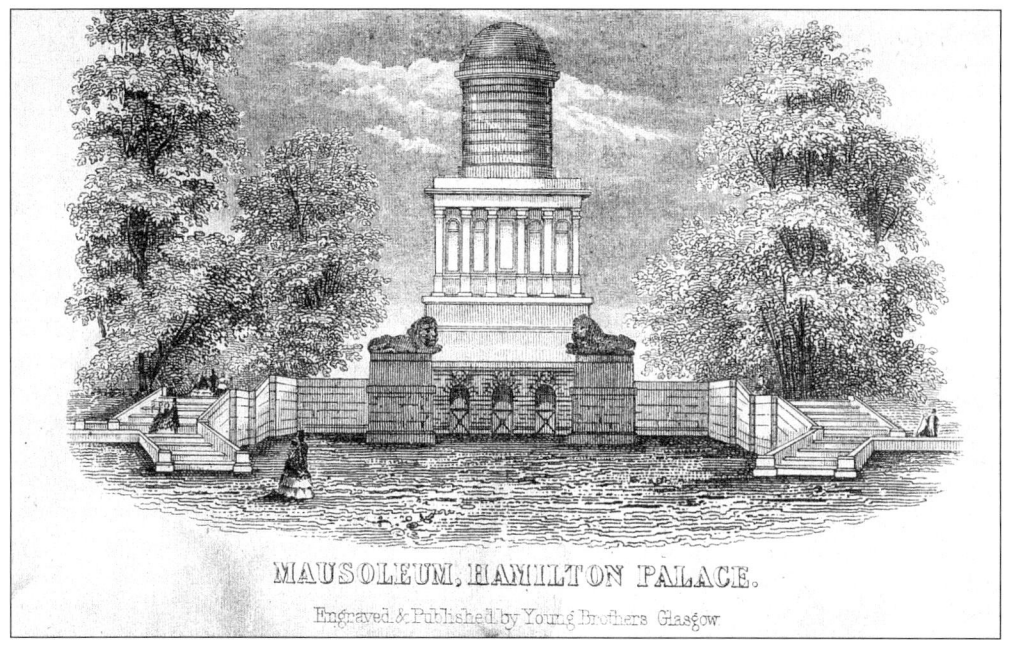

MAUSOLEUM, HAMILTON PALACE.
Engraved & Published by Young Brothers Glasgow

The Mausoleum, erected by the 10th Duke in 1845-1856, passed to the Burgh. It rests on foundations so deep that it simply sank twenty feet with little damage when the ground subsided. Bronze doors, a reduced replica of those of the Baptistry in Florence, with three of the five biblical scenes on each door, were removed after the subsidence and now lie inside. There is a remarkable echo for fifteen seconds when the doors are closed. When the bronze doors were in place, the echo lasted a record thirty-one seconds. At the rear is the entry to the vaults, protected by a pair of lions, one sleeping. After subsidence, the vaults were subject to flooding from the Clyde for some years, and more recently, when the Cadzow Burn was diverted during work on the new plans for the area, further flooding occurred. (*Above*: A contemporary etching by Young Bros., Glasgow, 1860; *below*: PPC, 'Caledonia Series,' c.1910)

Lion at Mausoleum, Hamilton

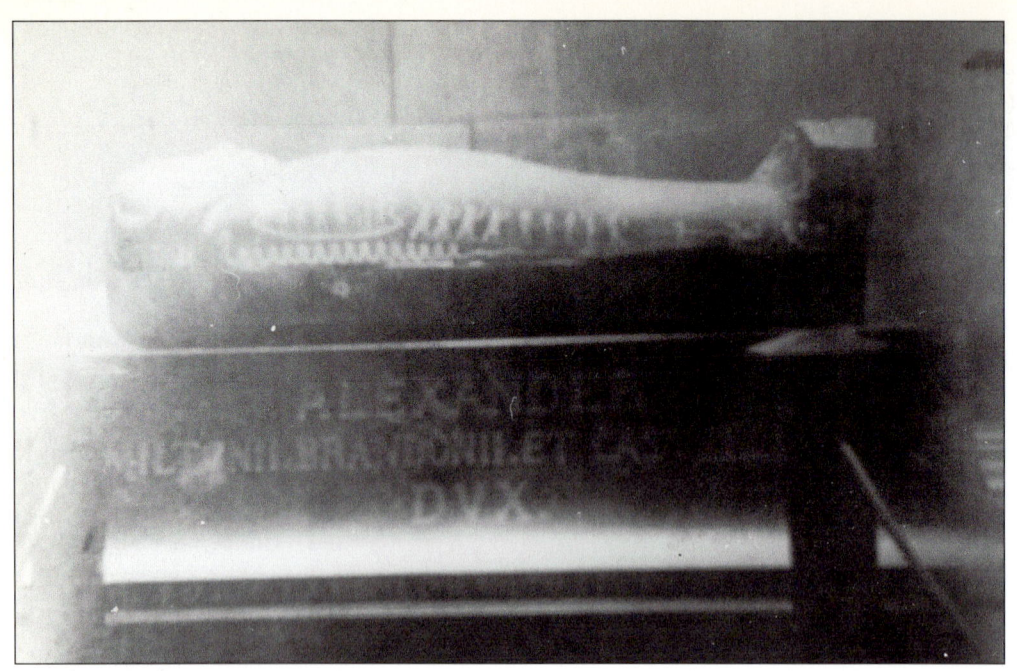

Alexander, 10th Duke of Hamilton, at rest in his Mausoleum in the sarcophagus from Memphis after Princess Sarr had been evicted. He remained here until the twenties and was then buried, in his sarcophagus, in the Bent Cemetery a mile or two away where he remains, with others of the family. The Duke was taller than the mummy, so, on his previous instructions, his legs below the knee were removed and fitted in to grooves cut in the sides of the sarcophagus.

The Avenue and Mausoleum. The Avenue, a double line of oaks, led through the estate, to the Palace and then to Chatelherault, via the Avon Bridge, over three miles in all. A few trees survive beyond the Avon and that section of the Avenue has been replanted. (PPC, 'Caledonia Series,' c.1910)

The 13th Duke, with the Duchess and their eldest son, the infant Marquis of Clydesdale (1903-1973), perhaps in his christening robe. The sender of this 1903 postcard writes 'Isn't she pretty, *n'est ce pas?* I doubt she won't be able to nurse much in a gown like that.'

This postcard shows the Duchess, a proud mother, with the Marquis and three younger children: Jean, Margaret and Nigel, Earl of Selkirk (1906-1997.) In Stother's 1910-1911 Annual the children are highly praised, '.... a very pretty quintette.... they are exceedingly healthy, and are possessed of more than average brain-power.' (PPC, John Mein, 1909)

Dungavel House, on the far side of Strathaven, the Ducal Lanarkshire home after leaving the Palace. In later years it became an open prison. Recently, due to pressure on accomodation elsewhere, it has been less 'open.' (PPC, A. Morton, Strathaven)

Ross House, a rambling Victorian mansion in red sandstone, by the junction of the Avon and the Clyde. A bridge across the Avon from Motherwell Road has long gone and the only access today is by private roads from Ferniegair. It is still lived in and is well hidden in the trees. Casual visitors to the estate are no longer welcome. (PPC, 'Wrench Series', *c.*1905, K.Norris Collection)

The Hamilton Caledonian Bowling Club (founded 1891), is beside the tennis courts in Motherwell Road, where the great new roundabout is. The move here from the Old Town was in 1911 and the Clubhouse and greens are brand new in this view. Subsidence caused problems in 1943 but these were overcome. The town's oldest club, the Hamilton, dates from 1841 and moved to Strathmore Road in 1881. (PPC, 'Caledonia Series,' 1911)

Lanarkshire Tramways Company's first route, Wishaw-Blantyre, opened on 22 June 1903. Car No. 20 was on a trial run, three days earlier, between Motherwell and Hamilton, a route closed on 6 October 1930. (PPC, 'Brandon Series')

The Old Bridge on the road to Motherwell crossed the Clyde where the Avon joined it. Built in 1780, it was replaced in the 1930s by the present one, straightening out the kink in the old route. The trams crossed it and the tall gantry held the overhead wires which stretched to the other side. (PPC, Rapid Photo Co., V276-4, c1910)

The remains of the old bridge were still around on the Motherwell bank until the M74 was built in 1966. The bathers here are enjoying themselves beside the 'new' bridge. (PPC, J.B. White Ltd, Dundee A6410, c.1951, reproduced by kind permission of Whiteholme (Publishers) Ltd)

Three
Cadzow Street

Cadzow Street was built as the Industrial Revolution gathered pace and new, faster transport links were needed for both people and goods in any part of the Kingdom hoping to join in the prosperity. The eighteenth century saw the canal system expand and new roads allowed speedier travel by coach to cut journey times. Much of this progress was possible thanks to the work of two Scots, John MacAdam and Thomas Telford, the latter building the new Glasgow-Carlisle highway, including, in 1825, Hamilton's Avon Bridge. Cadzow Street, connecting the Bothwell Road with the Carlisle Road, was approved in 1819 and completed in 1835, cutting out the steep gradients and awkward corners of the old Muir Street-Castle Street route. Ironically, before long, most of the traffic south was going by rail, anyway. Cadzow Street in time rivalled Quarry Street for shopping, and beyond the bridge over the Cadzow Burn it became a place for offices, banks and some substantial villas, as well as the Roman Catholic Church. Earlier this century the handsome new Town Hall and library were completed. One plot, opposite the Town Hall, was never built on and very recently it became a car park. Legend has it that it was on this land that the victims of a cholera epidemic were buried. By the fifties, Cadzow Street was becoming very busy with through traffic and by 1967, before the M74 at last by-passed the town, it was often a nose-to-tail experience. New shopping habits in the present era have affected its role and some years ago the one-way traffic system cut the street in two. Change never ceases, and Cadzow Street will soon no longer be part of a main traffic route.

Cadzow Street before the Second World War. The trams were well established and profitable; No. 45 is about to turn left down Keith Street 'en route' to Newmains. The barman at the Castle Street corner is keeping the pavement clean. Take away the tram, and its poles and the energetic barman, and not a lot has changed. (PPC, 'Caledonia Series', c.1912)

By the 1950s traffic was increasing all the time. At the Castle Street corner was the Commercial Bank of Scotland, which later merged with the Royal Bank. Beyond were Graham's and House of Johnston (both furniture & furnishings) and Lightbody's (Bakers and Confectioners) tearoom, where, in those more leisured days, many of the local GPs met for morning coffee. (PPC, Valentine D1608, 1956)

John Dick, the newsagent, was still at the Quarry Street corner in the mid-1960s. City Bakeries' tearoom was just past Getty's leather goods shop. Crossing behind the B-registration (1964) Wolseley 1500 car is a young man with long hair – a portent of fashion changes to come. (PPC)

Church Street crosses Cadzow Street in the foreground and the Cross is in the distance. The buildings are recognisable today, if not the transport. Church Street leads down from the left to Grammar School Square and up a short way to the main entrance to the old parish church. The tram is bound for Wishaw. (PPC, Valentine, 22422, c.1905)

Looking up Cadzow Street at the Campbell Street crossing. On the left, Campbell Street led to Chapel Street and the New Cross, but it now forms part of the wide Leechlee Road, which divides here to send its traffic either up or down Cadzow Street. This peaceful afternoon in 1937 shows the Cadzow Bar (left) selling Maclachlan's Castle Ales, and opposite is the Hamilton Radio House (still trading in Quarry Street) advertising Murphy radios. Peter Wyper & Sons' shop is beyond it and Lightbody's has the clock. Lawson's stationers at the corner stock Player's, Wills' Capstan and Mitchell's Prize Crop cigarettes. Glasgow's Mitchell Library was built thanks to a bequest by Stephen Mitchell. The trams have gone and a Central SMT bus is now approaching. (PPC, Valentine, A6086, 1937)

The old parish church, the replacement for the Collegiate Church by the Palace, was designed by William Adam and built in 1734. The lantern was added in 1841. Standing inside the gates since 1926 is the ancient Netherton Cross, moved here from the Low Parks. Four Covenanters, executed in the seventeenth century, lie in the churchyard. (PPC, Valentine)

Cadzow Street between the bridge and the Cross in 1956. Left, part of the 1901 'Keith' building, the handsome red sandstone premises of the grocer and provision merchant who gave his name to the new street at the Old Cross in 1903. Keith's truck is standing at the shop further along the street. The business closed in the 1960s. (PPC, Valentine, D1609)

Looking from Church Street to the bridge, library and town hall. John Smith, on the right of the photograph, was a wool shop and The Household Supply Company on the left is next to Rodger, tobacconist, whose shop is now a post office. In the distance is the British Linen Bank at the corner of Auchingramont Road. (PPC, Valentine, D8123, 1963)

The Cadzow Burn runs from behind Peacock Cross, under Union Street and through the Old Town on its way to the Clyde. The bridge was widened in 1901 for the trams. A plaque commemorates the Battle of Heiton, fought between the Covenanters and Cromwell's men in 1650. (PPC, Cynicus Publishing Co., Tayport, 1904)

The new Hamilton Kilwinning Masonic Lodge No. 7 in course of construction, with St Mary's church beyond. The earlier lodge had been taken down when Keith Street was opened. The new lodge, like that of many other buildings in the town, was the work of local architect Alexander Cullen. The town hall and library were still to come. (PPC, 'Caledonia Series,' 1904)

A tram for Blantyre approaches Auchingramont Road. The new Masonic Lodge is shown to good advantage. The Royal Bank of Scotland, on the left, was separated from the Bank of Scotland by the 'cholera' field. (PPC, Valentine 46142, 1904)

43

The new library, another Alexander Cullen building, opened in 1907, not long before this photograph was taken. The Royal Bank on the left dates from 1871. (PPC, 'Caledonia Series')

The United Free church in Auchingramont Road was replaced by flats in the 1960s, which did not please all in this exclusive avenue of stately Victorian villas. The Congregational church met the same fate after union with that in Park Road. The North British Railway Station was directly behind the church until the line closed in the 1950s. 'That is Storey in the cart' according to Mrs Storey who sent the card. (PPC, 'Brandon Series,' 1903)

The original design for Alexander Cullen's town hall and library. When built, the central dome was left out and the towers were given small domes instead of pyramid or 'pokey hat' finials. The Municipal Offices were opened by King George V on 5 July 1914. (PPC, 'Brandon Series' c.1902)

The library and town hall from Cadzow Bridge. The Bridge is high above the Cadzow Burn and the well-laid out little park below the right parapet (reached by steps beside the library, through some decorative metalwork) is now connected with a newly made path along the wooded banks on the other side of the bridge. (PPC, Valentine, A6085, 1937)

45

L.S.Smellie & Sons have been auctoneers and valuators since the firm was founded in 1874 by Lawson Stewart Smellie, whose great-grandson Robert Smellie carries on the tradition. The cattle market moved to Strathaven in 1990 but the weekly furniture mart and quarterly antiques sale continues in what was once the Muir Street Relief church, built in 1761. Looking down Lower Auchingramont Road (once known as Mary Moore's Brae, after the old gatekeeper of Auchingramont House) the fields across Muir Street were used for the cattle to be grazed while they waited to be sold. The Mote Hill housing estate was built here a few years ago. Holy Cross High School and the student quarters of the former Teacher Training College (now private apartments) are top left. The house in the foreground is now an Indian restaurant.

Robert Smellie, son and successor of the founder of the firm, played football for Queen's Park from 1885-1895 in the days when the amateurs made up the national team. He was president of the club in 1910-1911 and had played for Hamilton Athletic at the age of fifteen.

ROBERT SMELLIE,
Past President, 1910-1911.
Prominent Player, 1885-1895.

Alex Smellie (1902-1979) was a highly respected, forthright citizen of Hamilton. As auctioneer and valuator he was known, not just in Lanarkshire, but throughout Scotland, the North of England and Ireland for his skill, his fairness and his no-nonsense approach to business. He was a member of Hamilton Golf Club, and four times Club Champion with a handicap of +2. Those who knew him personally testify to his humour and generosity.

The Christmas Poultry Sale on 15 December 1961. Jim Strachan is the auctioneer, Robert Smellie holds up the turkey and James Law is the clerk.

The old Lanarkshire Miners' County Union offices at 116, Cadzow Street, another Cullen building, of 1907. Over the doorway is a carving of clasped hands. The Union was founded in the 1870s at a time of great unrest in the mines, with Keir Hardie, a miner in Quarter, as secretary. Robert Smellie from Larkhall, president when this letter was written during the First World War, was a well known political figure from the 1880s until the collapse of the General Strike in 1926. 'Dear Sir, I had a conversation with Mr Sorbie about a benefit concert. He advised me to write and ask you. As you are aware perhaps I'm busy sending out "—— Black" to Scottish Soldiers. Perhaps you could give a concert for funds for this object. Yours sincerely, J.Robertson. P.S. You could see Mr Sorbie.' The addressee is not named. John Robertson was well known for his battles on behalf of fellow miners in Hamilton in the 1890s.

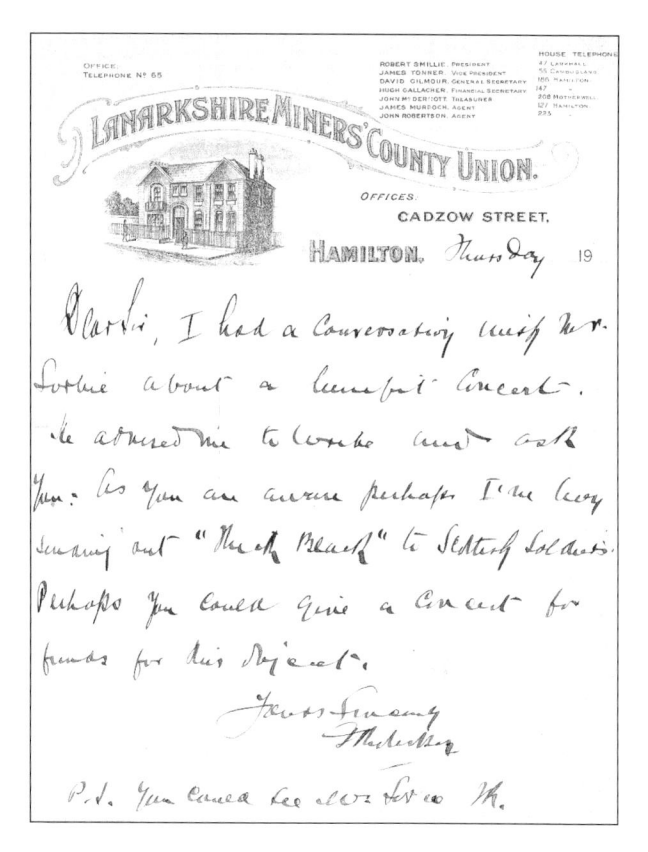

A postcard from a set illustrating life in the Lanarkshire mines, published by the proprietors of the Hamilton Herald.

St Mary's Roman Catholic church, near the top of Cadzow Street. Irish immigration from the 1780s onwards resulted in the Hamilton Mission being established in 1843 and funds were raised by the community to allow the present church to be built. The early years were difficult with few priests lasting the pace (one was found to be 'too corpulent for mission work'), but Michael Conder, 1850-59, enterprising and vigorous, gave the church much-needed stability. The Duchess of Hamilton, who had converted to the Catholic faith in 1850, was supportive of the then largely working-class congregation. The church building was recently cleaned and restored, and continues to flourish today. (PPC, 'Brandon Series.' Historical data obtained from St Mary's Hamilton, A Social History, 1846-1996, edited by Thomas Devine, published by John Donald.)

Cadzow Street merges with Muir Street at the top of the hill. The Catholic church is behind the Sir John Watson Fountain and modern flats have replaced the house which once stood behind the fountain. A horse-drawn cart is using the tram track for an easier climb, probably to the annoyance of the tram driver. (PPC, Cynicus Publishing Co.)

Four
Bothwell Road and Almada Street

The road to Bothwell Bridge became, in 1934, Hamilton's first dual carriageway, but its history goes back to 1722 when the Town Council paid Adam Weir of Whistleberry to improve on the path by the Clyde. Boggy ground, increasing traffic and disputes about funding though, kept it always in a poor state of repair. In 1950 it was described as 'the worst road in Lanarkshire' and not until 1966, when the motorway had taken away the through traffic, was it rebuilt, the Council having refused to do so because it received no 'trunk route' subsidy. The Duke's estate was one side of the road and at the Hamilton end was Gallowshill, a name needing no explanation – now a roundabout marks the spot. The Battle of Bothwell Bridge in 1679 has an important place in Scottish history. The private Hamilton College replaced the short-lived teacher training college and there can be seen a little of the Palace Grounds' decorative cast-iron railings, moved from Motherwell Road. The rest of that side of Bothwell Road is devoted to the motor trade, Hamilton Racecourse and the Animal Welfare centre. On the other side Hamilton Home, otherwise known as the poor house, has gone, but handsome Victorian villas and a public house survive in one form or another, as does the public park. The rest is an industrial estate with the Strathclyde Fire Brigade's Headquarters near the bridge. New housing is appearing on undeveloped sites, including part of the racecourse car park. Almada Street's name dates from the Napoleonic wars. The area between it and Muir Street is an interesting mix of old housing of all sorts, backed by a mature post-war Council housing estate. Here too, are the North Church of Scotland and the old baths, now a listed building that is to become a museum, while a splendid new Water Palace has replaced it in Almada Street. The Barracks have been replaced by Bell College, perhaps to be the University of Hamilton one day. Almada Street, dominated by the County Buildings, has been largely rebuilt but the wide Clydesdale Street is still lined by dignified Victorian villas for much of its length. Here too, was Douglas Park, the home of Hamilton Academicals FC, and now a retail park. The Accies supporters wait hopefully for their new stadium.

The Barracks in Almada Street, and along Bothwell Road to May Street, was the Regimental Depot of the Cameronians (Scottish Rifles) from 1881, when the 26th joined the 90th Perthshire Light Infantry in the new Regiment and the former Cavalry Barracks became the Regimental Depot. The Cameronians, disbanded in 1968, had a long list of Battle Honours from 1690 on. The view of the Sergeants' Mess (opposite page) dates from the days of peace but the scene at the Barracks Gate is of wartime with recruiting posters in plenty, before conscription was in force. The H.L.I. and the Cameronians are calling for volunteers and one message reads 'Britain is Fighting for Freedom for Europe and to Defend your Mothers, Wives and Sisters from the Horrors of War – Enlist Now.' To defend your womenfolk in the Scottish Rifles you had to be at least 61 inches tall. The Cameronians' Museum is beside the town Museum in Muir Street. (PPC, 'Caledonia Series', 1915)

The Sergeants' Mess, shortly before the First World War. (PPC, 'Herald Series', 1911)

Muirhall was the home of the Cameronians Territorials unil the 1970s; an imposing office block has replaced it. The tram is turning into Almada Street from Muir Street. The building just seen on the left survives as a row of shops to this day, although it was condemned a few years ago. (PPC, 'Brandon Series' 1904)

The Sheriff Court, Almada Street at Beckford Street, or 'County Buildings' when it was also the Burgh and County offices. Built in 1835, it was modified and enlarged in the 1880s. The street names commemorate the action at the fortress of Almeida in the Peninsula War, and the family name of the 10th Duke of Hamilton's wife. Much the same outside, inside it is regrettably as busy as ever. (PPC, Wrench Series' 7008, *c.*1904)

Beckford Street. Beckford Lodge at the far end was a maternity hospital but is now used for clinics and offices. Beyond the court are the Community Health offices. The houses on the left were replaced by Council offices in the 1930s. (PPC, 1919, J.Potter Collection)

The modern County Buildings, Almada Street, opened by Queen Elizabeth, the Queen Mother, in 1964, were designed by the County Architect, D.G.Bannerman, whose office blocks in Beckford Street were at one time planned to extend right round Almada Street, Douglas Street and Clydesdale Street. The building is reminiscent of the UN Building in New York, a resemblance that was not accidental. The circular debating chamber on the left was unused for many years due to successive re-organisations, but as this is now the administrative heart of South Lanarkshire District Council it has regained its function. Unlike many buildings of the time, it has worn well. (PPC, Valentine, D8673, 1964)

A view of the County Buildings from Barnsley Street, which disappeared altogether before the 1970s. On the left are the electricity offices.

55

Hamilton Athletic, later Hamilton Academicals, a Scottish Junior League team in 1896. President of the club and Provost of Hamilton, Robert Smellie (see p.47) stands on the extreme left of the back row.(Picture by kind permission of Stuart Marshall)

The Public Park, Bothwell Road, laid out in 1894, courtesy of the Duke and James Dixon, coalmaster. Not very accessible from most parts of the town, it has suffered like most others of its kind from loss of popularity. When first opened, though, weekends and holidays would see it well used in good weather and it is easy to visualise the trams unloading crowds at the gate in Edwardian days. The war memorial is the scene of the Remembrance Day services. (PPC, 'Herald Series' 1936)

The park has a modern children's playground at the New Park Street entrance and the bandstand, which brought 'music to the masses' when such delights were less accessible, is well maintained. The floral display must have been a delight in previous years. (PPCs: *Above*: Valentine 205996, 1929; *Below*: 'Philco Series' 4029, Edwardian)

Hamilton Wednesday was one of those local amateur football teams who took their name, like the more famous Sheffield club, from the day of their weekly match. (PPC, Margaret Graham Collection)

Hamilton Park Racecourse, sometime fancifully described as the 'Ascot of Scotland.' There has been racing in the town for over two centuries and the present Hamilton Park was laid out in 1926, the previous one, like everything else in the Palace grounds, having subsided. The course is well attended with seventeen days of racing in the year, including the Saints & Sinners meeting in summer. (PPC, Valentine A6090, 1937)

Bothwell Bridge from the Hamilton bank of the Clyde. The Battle of Bothwell Bridge in 1679 saw the Duke of Monmouth rout the Covenanters, who are commemorated in the monument on the Bothwell bank. Two trams are about to pass: the 'outside' deck of one is busy, with just one passenger 'inside.' In the early days, the long round trip from Hamilton via Uddingston, Bellshill, New Stevenston and Motherwell, was a popular excursion on fine evenings or weekends. In the twilight the double seat was a handy place for a little 'spooning,' as seen below. In later years, the back seat of the cinema proved to be even better suited, with both privacy and warmth. (PPCs: published by Park, Stationer, Bothwell, 1913; 'Living Picture Series')

59

Bothwell Bridge, and a lady cyclist could safely ignore the rules of the road. It is much busier now, but nothing compared to the expressway from Blantyre and East Kilbride which passes under it, through the arch on the Hamilton bank of the Clyde. (PPC, published by Park, Bothwell, 1910)

In the thirties this litle park was laid out into an attractive riverside garden. It survived to some extent until the Expressway was built, but Bothwell Bridge today is not a very peaceful place for those on foot. (PPC 'Herald' Series)

Five
New Cross to Low Waters

The New (or Top) Cross, dates from the 1840s, when Duke Street was formed. Earlier, the Nolt Market, for cattle and horses, was here. Above the Cross, the road climbs for three miles to a height of over 700 feet, past Low Waters, Eddlewood and Limekilnburn, and towards Strathaven. Central Station was opened in 1876 when the Duke finally allowed the Caledonian Railway to extend from the old Barracks (now Hamilton West) terminus. The new line split both Orchard Street and Park Road in two, after unsatisfactory bridges built at the time were removed. The goods yard along Brandon Street was replaced by the bus station when the service was electrified in the early 1970s. Old sandstone tenements and villas still line the narrow streets immediately above the Cross, as do some surviving weavers' cottages and small workshops. Brown Street (named after a local builder) and Johnstone Street were demolished around 1970. The Silvertonhill estate had passed from the Dukes to another branch of the Hamiltons in the fifteenth century and then to the Weirs. Waird Lodge, at the corner of Chatelherault Crescent, stood for some years after the private housing was built in the 1960s, marking the Duke's rightful access to the High Parks, a right confirmed in a Court of Session action in 1873. Hamilton spread uphill along and around the road to Strathaven, but until after the First World War and the start of council house building, there was plenty of open space above Burnblea Street, before the little hamlet of Low Waters was reached. Since then housing has spread on each side of the road, with much private building and private ownership of council property transforming the scene.

The Proclamation of George V, King Emperor, at the New Cross on Tuesday 10 May 1910, the platform party tightly corralled in front of the Town Hall. The procession, in which the military, regular and territorials were strongly represented, assembled in Chapel Street (site of the New Cross Centre now) and marched down to Cadzow Street and back up Quarry Street. Edward VII had been proclaimed at the Old Cross, but the ceremony was moved so as not to interrupt the trams. The spectators in the Brandon Street crowd behind the soldiers and the all-male official party stand for Provost Pollock to read out the proclamation precisely at the last stroke of 12 noon on the Town Hall clock. Hugh Young, in a message on this postcard to his Aunt Jeanie, writes 'the crowd on the platform are the members of the Council and the clergy etc. All the 'heid yins' of the town seem to have been there.' King Edward had been popular and a Day of Mourning was held in the town ten days later.

Brandon Street (named from the Duke's English title) in 1938. The Town Hall clock shows half-past two. The post office looks much the same today but now announces itself in Technicolor plastic. An old-fashioned gas lamp survives across from the parked car with 'L' plates. Traffic lights have arrived at the New Cross. (PPC, Valentine A6792)

Brandon Street in the early 1970s when this stretch was briefly dual carriageway, which it may become once more after many years of one-way traffic. Baird's department store has replaced the Town Hall. (PPC, published by Whiteholme, 4330W, reproduced by courtesy of Whiteholme (Publishers) Ltd)

63

Brandon United Free church was built when the street was opened in 1831, and the cast of the children's Operetta *The Hours* is seen here with 'Old Father Time.' The girls in the front row are holding the Moon, two Stars and a Diamond. The congregation united with Avon Street church in 1970 to form St Andrew's when the site was needed for the bus station. (PPC, 1905)

Hamilton Grammar School goes back to the Middle Ages but the building in Auchincampbell Road dates from 1913. The school was known as Hamilton Academy from 1848 until it reverted to the old name after merging with St John's Grammar School in 1972. It has had a distinguished academic record and the building was recently refurbished and extended.

The New Cross, 1932. The Town Hall stands up straight, before the steeple started to lean into Duke Street. The Egg Marketing Co., Ltd., with just one thing to sell, is between the Royal Hotel and the Athletic Vaults. (PPC, Valentine 217165)

The Royal was owned by G. Dodd, as all could see. He and his wife stand at the door. The building looks much the same today but is now divided into apartments. The Royal Bar became a bank but is now a shop for those planning to be wed. (PPC, 'Brandon Series' 1903)

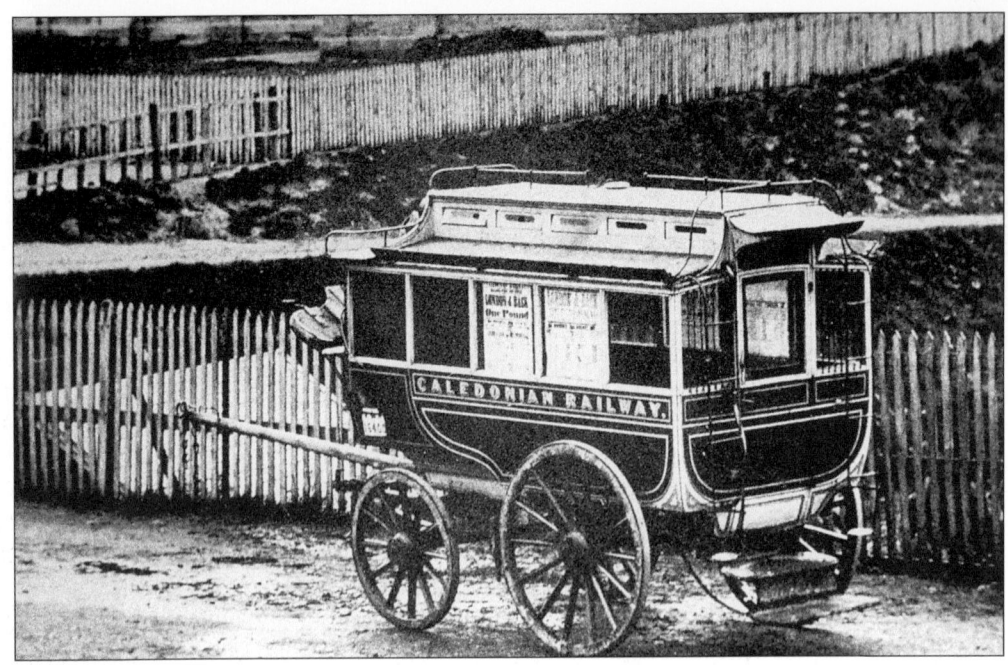

Until 1876 the Caledonian Railway line from Glasgow ended at Hamilton West (then known as Barracks Station) and a horse bus took passengers into town. The posters advertise 'London & Back – One Pound.' (Photograph, c.1870, reproduced by courtesy of South Lanarkshire District Council)

Central Station, from where you could until the 1960s catch a train not merely to Glasgow, Motherwell and Coatbridge but to Larkhall, Stonehouse, Strathaven and Coalburn too. The late Tom Fraser, MP for Hamilton, had the painful job, as Minister of Transport, of approving these Beeching cuts. Trains to Larkhall are promised to run again – maybe. (PPC 'Philco Series,' 2858, c.1916)

The Caledonian Railway's Central Station opened in August 1876 and a celebratory dinner was held on the 25th, when Mr Kirkpatrick, the stationmaster, declared that he would 'rather face a crowd of tumultuous passengers than give a speech'. Nevertheless, he carried on speaking for some time. The military have arrived back, possibly from their annual parade held in the summer. The buildings are not yet blackened by soot-they were demolished in the early 1970s when the line was electrified. A much smaller booking office was built and the original gas lighting was also replaced. The booking office in Kemp Street, now disconnected, remains as business premises.(Photograph reproduced by courtesy of South Lanarkshire District Council)

Quarry Street from the New Cross. It curves past Central Station and Kemp Street, named after the builder Baillie Kemp. The domed building, where the stationmaster's house had been, was known as Templehall. (PPC, Valentine, 80928, 1915)

Quarry Street from Gateside Street. Avon Street is on the right and the Victoria Bar at the corner is still in business under the same name. The Victoria Hall, now Messrs Stepek's shop, was a music hall where Harry Lauder, who once lived round the corner in John Street, first trod the boards. Most buildings seen here remain today. (PPC, published by G. Buchanan, New Cross, 1916)

Woodside Walk, an ancient street, led to Woodside House, where Claverhouse is said to have stayed on the eve of the Battle of Bothwell Brig. Carlton Court and Hilton Court replaced it in the 1960s. The Peter Macarthur tartan mill (1921) was originally a biscuit factory. The spire and roof of Cadzow parish church are seen on the right before Gateside Street is reached. A wintry scene from the 1970s.

The Lauder family lived in this cottage in John Street when Harry was a miner. It was taken down when a builder's yard opened on the site, beside the old bridge from James Street over the railway.

Gateside Street at Brown Street, looking up to Portland Place and Low Waters Road in the 1910s. On the right, the Butterburn Inn is followed by the gasworks across Burnside Lane, opposite Johnstone Street. The building on the left was taken down when Johnstone Road was built to connect with Silvertonhill Avenue. When trams were introduced to Hamilton in 1903, the Burgh Council sought permission to run their own line up the hill to Low Waters but it never happened.

Miners' rows were a common sight. Steps led to two separate one or two-room houses and the doors below opened off a close from the front of the building to the rear behind the steps. Sanitary facilities were basic. This row was one of many crowded together on either side of Strathaven Road, just above Cadzow Bridge. They were demolished in the 1950s. (Photograph reproduced by kind permission of South Lanarkshire District Council)

Looking down Low Waters Road from above Jack Street in 1880. Low Waters, an ancient name, was perhaps a corruption of 'Low Quarter.' In 1879 Keir Hardie ran a tobacconist's here, while his mother ran a grocery business. (Photograph reproduced by kind permission of South Lanarkshire District Council)

A view from Cadzow Bridge twenty years later shows houses on either side of the road which survive to this day. The bridge carried the road over the rails to Cadzow pit. When the pit closed a metal window factory took the site, then Rolls-Royce. When they left, the line was lifted and the bridge went, but the name persists. An industrial estate where hearing aids are made is here now. (PPC, 'Brandon Series')

Lovers' Lane is said to have run from Tuphall Road to Mill Road. The mature Edwardian lovers are set to cross the foaming Cadzow Burn by the present-day Fairhill Road. The mill was by Chantinghall House, where Nethan Court was built around 1980. (PPC, 1907)

The Whisky Well gave the only water the local laird, Sir John Watson, Bart would put in his whisky. The house, built in 1873 on Neilsland Road by the post office, survives, but the well by the burn at the bottom of the garden does not. The conical post marked the gateway to the well. (PPC, 1907)

Six
The Outskirts

Beyond the town centre, along Carlisle Road, is the village of Ferniegair and then, going south and west, a line would curve round Chatelherault, Quarter and modern housing estates, before reaching the outskirts of Blantyre. Much of this land was outside the Burgh boundary, which disappeared when the now defunct Strathclyde Region was born in 1975. Until after the Second World War, it was mostly open country with farms, some substantial mansions and coal mines or their wastelands. Townhead Street meets Duke Street at Broken Cross, where Barncluith Road branches off and then a wide stretch of Carlisle Road displays a variety of homes from douce thirties bungalows to dignified villas, low-lying private estates and the ultimate in spectacular urban living. The Old Avon Road leads to the original crossing of that river and a path to Chatelherault, the Dukes' hunting lodge, or, as the 5th Duke called it, his 'Dogg Kennel'. Threatened by extraction of sand almost up to its doors, it was saved for posterity in the 1970s after the estate passed to the Hamilton Council, and is the centrepiece of a Country Park. Quarter, another old mining village, now boasts a growing array of des. res. on its windswept site, with a grand view of the Clyde Valley. Eddlewood, Meikle Earnock, Fairhill, Laighstonehall, Little Earnock and Hillhouse are estates perpetuating ancient names and giving a cross-section of changing styles and building methods in local authority housing from the 1930s on, and they are nearly all now in good shape. The railway from Blantyre to Strathaven passed through this area until the 1960s.

Low Patrick Street, named 200 years ago after Alexander Patrick's estate, meets Townhead Street opposite Staneacre House. It was widened for the one-way system and the houses on the right were later replaced by a car park and filling station. Now the car park and Kwik-Fit at the end of the street have vanished as the traffic reverts to two-way. Motherwell lies beyond the Clyde and the M74. (Photograph by the author, 1976)

Miller Street was a route to Duke Street and the New Cross, before becoming a cul-de-sac. A doctors' surgery now fills the gap beyond the tenement, itself taken down. Barncluith School is at the junction in the distance. An annex to the school across Miller Street, later used for pupils with learning difficulties, has been replaced by modern flats. (Photograph by the author, 1976)

Broken Cross, where Quakers are known to have met in houses in the early eighteenth century, as it was in 1903. The scene is not much changed today. Robert McGhie's van (pastrycook and confectioner, 42 Chapel Street, dining rooms at 37 Cadzow Street), is in front of the school, which was opened as Townhead in 1875 and was Barncluith Primary, the oldest in the town. It closed a few years ago to become, after smartening-up, the Barncluith Business Centre. From Carlisle Road, Miller Street is on the left and Townhead Street on the right. (PPC, Brandon Series.)

Barncluith House (sixteenth century) with its hanging gardens by the Avon, is an architectural treasure, largely hidden from view. The gardens, which Dorothy Wordsworth waxed lyrical about in 1803, are not now maintained; restoration of the whole estate, by a new owner a few years ago, came to an end when his business collapsed. Barncluith, originally a Hamilton family property, was ravaged by the Regent Morton pursuing a vendetta in 1579. John Hamilton, Commissary of Hamilton & Campsie, restored it, landscaped the gardens and built the terraces overhanging the Avon. In 1908 Barncluith was bought by James C. Bishop, a coalmaster who took good care of it, adding decorative stonework from the Palace in 1927. Sir Robert Lorimer wrote in 1899, 'Barncluith is quite unlike anything else....the most romantic little garden in Scotland.... In the twilight, destinies might be determined (here).' Early in 1999 a serious fire severely damaged the house. (PPC, 'Ideal Series')

Barncluith in the 1930s. The gateway on the left leads to the gardens, which overhang the Avon at an angle of 55 degrees. The hanging (or 'Italian') gardens, seen from the Avon, are now largely hidden from the opposite bank by bushes and trees, though they can be made out on winter days. A footpath along the Avon leads to Larkhall. (PPCs: 'Herald Series,' Valentine 215958, 1932)

The Three Bridges. The Hamilton-Motherwell railway bridge leads to a tunnel under Carlisle Road, built at the Duke's insistence. A few years ago an ammunition train was derailed in it and the Carlisle Road area was evacuated. Telford's Bridge over Carlisle Road is beyond the Avon Mill and the Old Avon Bridge is between the other two. (PPC, Valentine 217166, 1932)

The Old Avon Bridge, of uncertain age. Bonnie Prince Charlie crossed in 1746 and a mail coach fell through into the Avon in 1819, killing the coachman, a passenger and two horses. No wonder Telford's bridge was welcomed. Carlisle Road is on the horizon and the Old Avon Road curls round by the cottage, now replaced by a nursing home. Houses cover the fields. (PPC, Valentine 215701, 1932)

Avon Mill, in use within living memory, was burnt down by vandals in the 1960s. Telford's bridge is beyond. Plans to restore the Mill as a restaurant were turned down more than once and a few years ago the ruins disintegrated in a massive and mysterious explosion. (PPC, 'Herald Series,' 1932)

Ferniegair, strung along Carlisle Road. Trams to Larkhall ceased in 1928. The miners' rows in the distance went long ago but the pub by the tree on that side remains. An isolated tenement has been restored at the far end of the village and there is an attractive self-contained council estate across from Chatelherault and Hamilton Golf Club. Individual modern houses have appeared on the main road. (PPC, published by Mrs L. Campbell, Ferniegair, 1923; Julia McLeod Collection)

The established Ferniegair church in a 1905 view. The school nearby closed a few years ago, despite vigorous protests. (PPC, 'Brandon Series,' John Potter Collection)

Chatelherault, the Duke's hunting lodge, named from his French title, was an abandoned ruin until restored to its former glory in the 1970s and is now the centrepiece of a country park. As far as possible the gardens have been restored to their original pattern. (PPC, Valentine 80926, 1915)

Cadzow Castle was a royal residence; Alexander III who ruled from 1249 to 1286 left charters signed from 'castrum nostra de Cadehow.' Regent Morton, during his visit to Hamilton in 1579, dealt with it as he did with Barncluith. What's now left remains unsafe behind a security fence. When it was found that one couldn't see the ruins across the Avon from the Duke's room in Chatelherault, some extra ruins were added. (PPC, 'Caledonia Series,' 1904)

A surviving corner of the Castle, with a small arched entrance. This photograph was taken about thirty years ago when it was still possible to explore the ruins safely, provided you didn't venture too near the edge of the ravine.

The White Cattle, the Duke's unique herd, now split between Lennoxlove and Chatelherault. Of uncertain pedigree as they have at some time been cross-bred with the Chillingham herd and a Welsh herd, their dispersal ensures that the breed will not be wiped out by disease. They are standing by the remaining oaks of the old Cadzow Forest. Some of the trees survive today, possibly older than the ruined Castle, as the forest is said to have been planted by David I in the twelfth century. (Photograph taken by the late Robert McLeod Snr, 1920s)

The Duchess Nina Institute in Quarter, now a nursing home, keeps the original name. The Duchess was anxious to provide a counter-attraction to pubs in mining districts, and in the Institute, billiards, carpet bowls, books and papers, and refreshments could be had. There was a bowling green outside, opened on 24 September 1910 by Their Graces and the family, while the village was *en fête*.

Quarter, about three miles from the centre of Hamilton, has a history going back to the days of Robert the Bruce, who granted the lands of Eddlewood to Walter Fitzgilbert. 'Quarter' may be a corruption of his first name. This Edwardian view of the main street (Limekilnburn Road) shows the post office (left) and houses since replaced by the Council. (PPC, published by Ritchie, PO, Quarter)

The local school on Limekilnburn Road is still noted for the excellence of its pupils' performance and is little changed in appearance. The postcard was sent by Joan Reid in the mid-1920s to her teacher Miss Carmichael, hoping she would soon recover from her illness.

The Manse, Quarter

The handsome Quarter parish church manse. The church was damaged by fire a few years ago but has been restored.

Above and opposite: Bonspiel at Limekilnburn in the 1920s. Curling nowadays is more likely to be found at the rink in the Low Parks. Many of the curlers here were miners from the local pits. In the 1930s, air shows were held at Limekilnburn, sponsored by the Duke of Hamilton. (Photographs taken by the late Robert McLeod Snr, 1920s)

Broomknowe Farm, off Brackenhill Road in Meikle Earnock, with the ploughman at work in the fields in the 1920s. The main farm buildings survive, somewhat modernized, but that at the right of the main block is a ruin. (Photograph by the late Robert McLeod Snr)

Townhead Cottage was on the path that led from Meikle Earnock at the top of Neilsland Road to Strathaven Road, where Eddlewood House once stood. The area is now largely occupied by modern houses. (Photograph by the late Robert McLeod Snr, 1920s)

Dykehead Infant School on Earnock Road. The back road to East Kilbride was undeveloped when the school was built in the 1930s at the instigation of Edward Flannigan. The local children had journeyed to school in Burnbank previously. The building now houses a bedding plant centre. (Photograph by A.E.Cunningham, 1970, reproduced by his kind permission)

Mid Stonehall (Alex. Cullen, FSA Scot, Architect) was built by John Watson in 1892 in place of the original Neilsland House and, in time, took that name itself. This entrance lodge was in the now closed stretch of Highstonehall Road and the site of the house has become Neilsland Park. The original house was near the top of the present Swisscot Drive, where there is now a pub. Swisscot is named after the Swiss cottage that was on the estate.

Earnock House, latterly the home of Sir John Watson, coalmaster, until his death in 1898. Modernised in 1874, the house was demolished in 1962. (PPC, 1907)

Curling at Torheads Lake on the Neilsland Estate in the 1920s, with the boathouse in the background. Beside Mrs Watson is Mr Hutcheson the chauffeur. Torheads was at the southern end of the estate, across from the Hamilton-Strathaven railway. In the early 1930s a hoax brought reporters and press photographers to Torheads after tales were planted of a Torheads Lake Monster. (Photograph by kind permission of Gordon Mitchell)

Woodfoot Cottage in 1909, looking towards Laighstonehall. The house stood by the bridge over the Earnock Burn, on what is still Woodfoot Road. At this point now, Sherry Drive, named after the then provost, climbs up to the 1970s Little Earnock housing estate and St Mark's Primary School. The card was posted by Mrs M.A. McLachlan to her sister, Mrs Vallance, a patient in Glasgow's Western Infirmary. Marion is the name of the little girl sitting on the parapet.

Comely Bank, Hillhouse, an estate built in the middle 1950s. Seen here when fairly new, the houses and gardens are well kept and tidy but as elsewhere it became, for a time, a less desirable address. With few shops nearby and few cars to go to non-existent supermarkets, vans provided most of life's necessities, as from the one in the mid-distance. Behind this street was then open land but private housing now stretches southward for a mile.

Seven
Burnbank

Burnbank became part of Hamilton in 1878, but still sees itself as a bit different. Peacock Cross (called after Mr Peacock, a crofter) dates from 1841 when the Cambuslang Road Trustees caused Union Street to be built and Burnbank Road to be improved. Industry included a foundry at the start of Wellhall Road (dealt with in the 1970s by the same juvenile who burnt down St John's Primary School) and the Hamilton Weaving Factory, here beside the railway from 1856. Burnbank Road is still lined on one side of its broad expanse with some impressive Victorian villas, while across the road were the Fulwood Foundry (now a small industrial park) and tenements. At Burnbank Cross the road now ends in a roundabout, and a bypass allows most traffic to speed past the heart of Burnbank without noticing. The centre was rebuilt in the early 1970s and not much is left from the old days except the churches, the ex-police station and the bingo hall. The division of the village into Burnbank and Greenfield has faded into history. Last century, the Greenfielders fought pitched battles in Glasgow Road with the Burnbankies, about what is not clear. It was in 1878 that the North British Railway came to Burnbank, but the station at Crawford Street was at first known as Greenfield. There was also plenty of heavy work in the district, but the Earnock pit closed in the 1950s and all the derelict land between Burnbank Cross and Hillhouse Road has been developed with housing and light industry. Then the Bolt Works and the Cable Works were followed into history by the modern carpet factory. The railway yards, with their wagon repair works, are partly overgrown and partly developed for housing. This happened in many places with compensating benefits and much healthier living conditions all round as the slums went and most houses were brought up to a good standard. Council estates, across the railway in Whitehill, on the Earnock pit site and along Farm Road, have had mixed fortunes over the years with general improvements taking place, while the Thorntree estate, built in the 1920s was always a 'good address' with hand-picked tenants. High Blantyre Road becomes Main Street at the old boundary with Blantyre, and Glasgow Road keeps its name as it crosses the Park Burn. The old Trades Hotel there, a well-run common lodging house, has become a builders' warehouse. Until the early 1970s it was a haven for dozens of homeless men, mostly elderly, and for many years under the benign supervision of Harry Doyle, but lack of modern fire and safety facilities led to its closure.

The Royal Visit, Monday 29 June 1953. Peacock Cross, and the Queen and Duke of Edinburgh will turn into Almada Street from Union Street on the left. Burnbank Road stretches into the distance and the gathering crowds are being marshalled by the police. The Peacock Bar is decked out, there are Union flags flying and a primary school crocodile is crossing to their place of viewing. The road sweeper ensures the royal limousine does not have to traverse unswept tarmac.

Her Majesty and the Duke enter Almada Street, past Peacock Cross Post Office and her cheering subjects. The royal couple wave from the open-backed Daimler. The cottages were later demolished and a new post office and Fyfe's funeral parlour built, while a tyre business took the rest of the site. The post office and shop disappeared not long ago.

The party's over and the crowds start to disperse. A 'Surf' van stranded outside the Bar had given a good view for some, as did other trucks. A tower wagon by the railway bridge on the right was even better. Police officers wait for the streets to clear and the buses in Burnbank Road wait too. It is a sunny summer day but judging by how the crowd is dressed, it can't be too warm. The royal visit had been a great success – one of the Queen's staff described her reception as the 'biggest, brightest and cheeriest yet.' She had entered the town to cheers from children lined up on the pavement who had good-humouredly booed the police escort that had led the royal car. Driving up Quarry Street and Union Street they reached the Town Hall via Almada Street. Major J.B.L. Monteith, Vice-Lieutenant of the County, greeted them and lunch was served in the Council Chamber. When Sir Alan Lascelles advised the Queen that it was time to move on to Motherwell, Her Majesty, according to the report in the *Hamilton Advertiser*, said she wasn't going anywhere until she'd had her coffee. The Duke was heard to remark that he was surprised to find Hamilton looking so bright and prosperous. (Photographs, including cover illustration, by the late Robert McLeod Snr)

Peacock Cross in the 1900s. The Peacock Bar survives, somewhat disguised in the modern manner. The Hamilton West church spire rises behind tram No. 2 on its way to Newmains.(PPC, published by Walter Benton, Glasgow, 'Unique Series')

Burnbank Road, beyond Peacock Cross, from the present day Linden Lea. The buildings on the right have been replaced. The Fulwood Foundry, beyond them, is now the site of the Fulwood business park, but villas hidden by the trees on the left have survived in one form or another. (PPC, published by Gray, Peacock Cross, 1910s)

Woodview Terrace, from Burnbank Road on 29 July 1981. The street party celebrated the marriage of the Prince and Princess of Wales and the red, white and blue pennants are flying.

A doctors' surgery at Burnbank Cross in 1970, with Mrs Elizabeth Jeffrey, the receptionist, in her cubby hole command post. The size of her office can be clearly seen. It held the medical records of over 6,000 patients but no telephone. The portable gas fire kept her and the patients warm. There was one other receptionist and a cleaner, but things have moved on since then!

Burnbank Cross from High Blantyre Road in the 1920s. All vanished in the early 1970s. It had been a busy junction with plenty of shops, an Italian cafe and an Italian fish and chip shop and always, as here, plenty going on. Forsyth's 'Fruit Bazaar' and the dairy nearby will still be remembered by many, but the fountain had gone earlier.

Looking to Burnbank Cross from Glasgow Road in the late 1960s. The newsagent, M.C. Dell, had recently moved from High Blantyre Road at the Cross. Templeton's was a famous Glasgow-based chain of grocers, swallowed up by Associated British Foods, along with Lipton and Galbraith. (PPC, J.B. White Ltd, Dundee, A9930)

96

Burnbank Cross, 1918. Tram track curves into Glasgow Road at High Blantyre Road where the Enfield Bar like the club bar (left) was here to the end. The Clydesdale Bank (centre) is still here, but in a modern building, being built (below) behind the original; the grocer's shop to its left latterly belonged to Mr Gibson, a well-known figure in Burnbank. (PPC, 'Herald Series' published by Anderson, 146 Glasgow Road, 1918; photograph 1975, by kind permission of A.E. Cunningham)

Glasgow Road from the Cross, on a summer afternoon, with Ann Street on the right. Beyond are the Plaza Cinema, hall, library and Gilmour Memorial church. The Plaza, now offering bingo, has been disguised behind a new front. (PPC, Valentine, D1617, 1956)

Glasgow Road at the railway bridge. Crawford Street, left, leads to Burnbank Station. The line opened on 8 May 1878 and from the Cadzow Street terminus of the Glasgow, Bothwell, Hamilton and Coatbridge Railway, North British or LNER passengers could later travel between all these places until the 1950s when the bridge over the Clyde became unsafe. (PPC, Valentine, 58924, 1907)

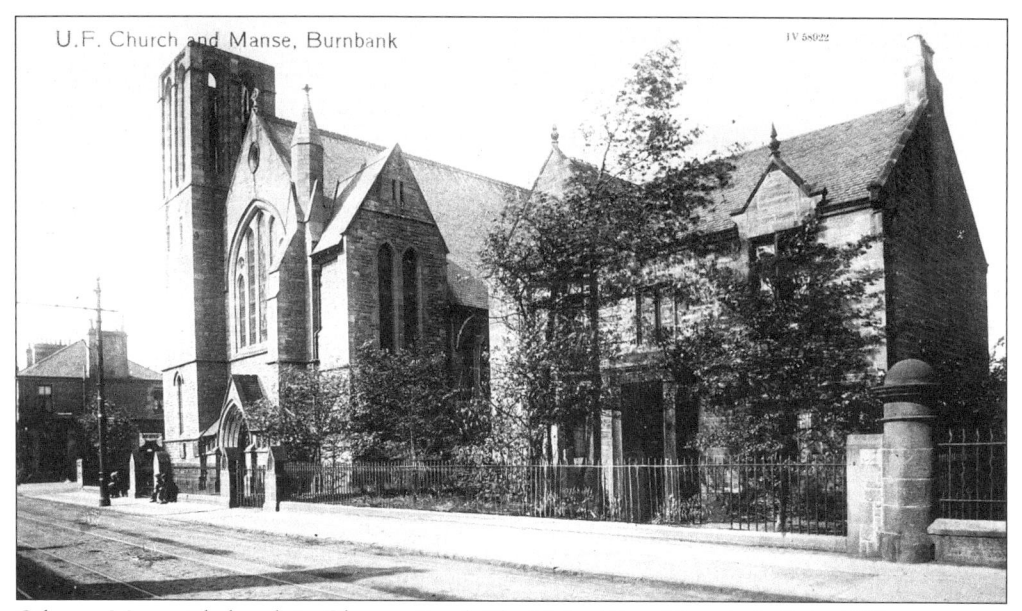

Gilmour Memorial church in Glasgow Road. The United Free Church, built in 1883, remains in use. Revd John Gilmour arrived in Hamilton in 1880 and the church was later given his name. The Burnbank Co-operative building is beyond the church. (PPC, Valentine, 58922, 1907)

Burnbank Athletic (Lanarkshire League Champions, 1895/96) played behind Greenfield School, by the MEA works. The 'Bumbees', so called with their black and yellow strips, had a moment of glory when they won the Junior Championship at Hampden in 1945. Cambuslang Rangers beat them but had fielded an unregistered player and Athletic won the replay 3-1. Going to Hampden, the Bumbees had a hard time in Cambuslang but that did not deter them from waving the cup aloft as their bus passed through on the way back. (Photograph by Sharp, Hamilton)

Burnbank parish church (built 1880) where Udston Road, on the left, branches off High Blantyre Road. Stewart Street, on the right, is now just a stub at this end. The church and houses survive but not the trees. The main road now feeds the East Kilbride Expressway and is busy enough to need traffic-calming measures. (PPC, published by William Love, Glasgow, 1922)

Udston Road at the top of Glenlee Street. A peaceful scene when the houses were new in the mid-1920s, showing to what a high standard the estate was built. The washing is hanging out to dry and a miner walks his whippet up Udston Road. (PPC)

Russell Street, in the same estate, at its junction with Udston Road (PPC)

High Blantyre Road from Russell Street looking towards Burnbank Cross, and with no traffic in this mid-1920s view. The sign on the kerb reads 'School – Drive Slowly' referring to the Roman Catholic School beside St Cuthbert's, the roof of which is seen. (PPC)

St Cuthbert Chapel at the corner of Reid Street and Glenlee Street. Russell Street is in the distance. Some happy children at the corner and a covered cart with three men and a horse – tinkers perhaps? (PPC, published by Dickson, newsagent, Burnbank, 1918)

The east end of Reid Street is a cul-de-sac and No. 10, then known as *Lilybank*, is near the end. The house looks very much the same today, only the car has changed.

The main part of Reid Street, looking back towards Glenlee Street, the line of neat cottages looking much as they do today. The children are coming home from school. (PPC, 1928)

Burnbank Methodist Church at the Glasgow Road end of Stewart Street, with two men on the roof starting demolition. (Photograph, 1970s, reproduced by kind permission of A.E. Cunningham)

Stewart Street in the 1960s, prior to demolition, looking to Burnbank Road with Reid Street crossing in the foreground. In the distance is the railway bridge with the roofs of Crawford Street beyond. (Photographs on this and next page reproduced by kind permission of A.E. Cunningham)

Glasgow Road in July 1972, with this row of shops and flats between Donaldson Street and Stewart Street about to be pulled down. Subsidence, as at the far end, was a problem throughout mining districts.

Flannigans' Bar. A. Cunningham, the last licensee, is the grandson of the original owner. Above, some youngsters are on a last inspection in March 1973, while, below, the pub and much else is just a memory. Edward Flannigan, a miner from Barrhead, came to Burnbank 100 years ago and later built the 'Railway Restaurant.' He died in 1928 and his daughter (Elizabeth Bonthrone Cunningham, music teacher and singer) and her husband ran the re-named 'Flannigans' Bar.' The restaurant re-opened in 1934 for a few years.

Walter McGowan, born in Burnbank on 13 October 1942, was boxing from the age of nine. British Flyweight Amateur Champion, he went on, in 1963, to win the British and British Empire Flyweight Championship after turning professional. Told that he had to be twenty-one to have a Lonsdale Belt, he, with Jack Solomons' help, successfully contested the ruling in the courts. He won the World title against the Italian, Salvatore Burunni, in 1966 and retired in 1971. Throughout his career he was trained by his ex-miner father, known to all as Joe Gans from the time he became a successful prizefighter at the booths in Hamilton and around. Joe (Thomas McGowan), who had once played football for Burnbank Athletic, adopted the name of the 'Barbados Demon,' the famous black American who won the World Lightweight Championship in 1902 and retained it for six years. A legend himself in the boxing world, no-one got the better of him when he was defending his son's interests, and verbal opponents usually retired after the first round. He died in 1986 at the age of seventy-two. Bobby Shearer, from Burnbank, the Rangers captain, looks on while Provost John Marshall and Celtic manager Jock Stein, another famous native of Burnbank, admire the belt. (Photograph and information courtesy of the *Hamilton Advertiser* and Walter McGowan MBE)

'Les 2e Artilleurs Alpins" march down a sunny Glenlee Street in May 1940, on their routine evening patrol. The company was billeted at Greenfield from May 1 but had soon to return to France when the Wehrmacht invaded their country. During their short stay they were given great hospitality by the Burnbank people which they never forgot, and when they departed from the station hundreds came to say goodbye and wish them good luck.

'Les Artilleurs' on a visit to Loch Lomond arranged by Robert McLeod. Father Joet, on the left, and Father Poquet beside him, with Robert McLeod Jnr between, were just two of many priests serving as combat troops in the regiment, as was Father Crespy on the right. Mr W. MacDonald, owner of Limetree Garage, is wearing a raincoat and the Colquhoun Estate lodge keeper makes up the group. (Photographs by Robert McLeod Snr, reproduced by kind permission of Robert McLeod Jnr)

107

Private Weir, Mechanical Transport Section of the 4th (Lanarkshire) Battalion, Home Guard in 1942. Above Udston, he is practising the 'rough stuff' in his motorcycle cross-country work before the critical eyes of his trainer. (Photograph by kind permission of A.E. Cunningham)

Burnbank from above the Foundry. A semi-rural scene from the turn of the century. Greenfield Foundry was later the site of Ireland's scrap metal yard off Glasgow Road by the Hamilton-Blantyre boundary. (PPC, Valentine c.1908)

Eight
Blantyre

No one is sure how Blantyre got its name – from St Blane, from the Gaelic for 'field of the holy men,' from the Welsh for a promontory, or (the Gaelic again) for 'a warm retreat,' you can take your pick. The Priory is recorded in the thirteenth century and its last vestiges survived to modern times. Ownership of the land depended on the fortunes and the whims of the sovereigns. James VI gave the lands and barony to Walter Stewart, the 1st Lord Blantyre, in 1599, and Blantyre became a burgh. More recently it was just a part of the 5th (later 8th) District Council of the County of Lanark but since 1975 Blantyre and Hamilton have shared the same Council. While David Livingstone is Blantyre's most famous son, Walter Stewart's daughter Frances had her image in everybody's pocket for 300 years as Britannia on our old pennies. Today's Blantyre was once three separate communities: Low Blantyre with the cotton mills and the Turkey Red works by the Clyde, Stonefield (along Glasgow Road), and High Blantyre. Like its neighbour, Blantyre became very much a mining centre and had its share of pit disasters. The residential districts have become much more attractive as many dingy pre-war and post-war estates that replaced old tenements and miners' rows have been brought up to date. Older houses remain throughout to give character to streets which also chart the development of local authority housing styles over the last seventy years, from the handsome 'Scandinavian' wooden houses by the Expressway roundabout, to the estate in High Blantyre, which seen from the Expressway, it looked, until the white box-like dwellings with flat roofs were modified, more like Beirut than Blantyre. More recent development has added to the mix of modern houses. Blantyre's two main streets, though, have gained nothing from modern redevelopment. After the twin railway bridges went and the Expressway came instead, Glasgow Road's rather shabby shops and dwellings were largely replaced as far as Station Road by a featureless line of industrial and domestic buildings set back from the road, the Sports Centre and a less than successful row of shops fronting the supermarket. Every junction has its mini-roundabout and Main Street in High Blantyre has fared no better. Light industries come and go, but on balance Blantyre has over the years succeeded in attracting a good mix, which together with local enterprises help to fill the industrial estates, from the original Main Street estate, where Rolls-Royce once was, to the modern, hi-tech estates not far from it.

Auchinraith Road, which connected Glasgow Road with High Blantyre. A peaceful scene with the Apothecary Hall by the lamp post. Latterly, it started with grim tenements and later there was council housing. The Expressway has taken away the junction with Glasgow Road. (PPC, c.1910)

Glasgow Road in 1903, at Logan Street. Stonefield church was later known as St Andrew's and burnt down in 1970 to be replaced by the present modern building. Most of the other buildings survived just a little longer. (PPC, Valentine, 41087)

Glasgow Road at Church Street, looking west. John Street is opposite, by John Forres' Castle Bar. A busy pre-war scene and the schoolgirl will have to be careful crossing the road. Nowadays, it is almost suicidal to do so, except on the pedestrian crossing by the shops. (PPC, Valentine, A6094, 1937, from an image in the St Andrews University Library)

At Logan Street in the early 1930s, a quieter afternoon for strolling across Glasgow Road. Since the 1903 view opposite was taken, the bar on the right had been built at Priory Place, the block which extended from Church Street. At John Street across the way was Marshall's the bootmakers. Logan Street now leads from Glasgow Road into the car park and is no longer a through route to Auchinraith Road.

Glasgow Road, looking east, the Picture Theatre with twice nightly shows. In later years it was all a continuous performance, which meant queuing in the rain and often seeing the end of the film before the beginning. This cinema opened in 1913. The sports centre replaced it. (PPC, Valentine A6093, 1937, from an image in the St Andrews University Library))

Tram No. 4, Hamilton, Motherwell and Wishaw Tramways Company (later Lanarkshire Tramways) just after the service opened on 22 July 1903. By 1907 Cambuslang was reached, linking up with Glasgow's trams. The last tram ran on 6 October 1930. The Blantyre terminus was just west of Stonefield Road, by Macdonald's bar, which was selling Tennent's Lager. (PPC, Valentine, 41086)

The park entrance in Glasgow Road, near Station Road. Victoria Street is on the right in the mid-distance, with the church at the corner. Most of the buildings seen here have gone, and the castellated public lavatories have been modernized. The long-armed tram standards remained in place long after the trams had gone. (PPC)

The Health Institute and Children's Welfare Centre in Victoria Street was built in 1928 and survives, minus its tower. It is used meanwhile as offices beside the modern Health Centre, itself a replacement for the original, which burnt to the ground shortly after being opened. (PPC)

Stonefield Road, with St Joseph's Roman Catholic School (since replaced by a flat-topped building of standard design) in Glasgow Road. It is a sunny Edwardian day with a pair of horses pulling a mighty load of baskets. At David Gibson & Sons Stonefield Store, the butter is a shilling a pound with cheese at the same price. John S. McCallum is a rival licensed grocer, while between their shops the Blantyre Co-op competes. The buildings on the right were taken down a few years ago, as were the houses on the left. Mrs Gormley's fruit and flowers shop on that side is the only surviving one. Modern housing has done away with the open space on the right and this scene is totally unrecognisable today. (PPC)

Blantyre Post Office at the foot of Stonefield Road during the First World War. Lord Kitchener (on the left window) appeals for 'More Men – God save the King', while on the other side are stationery and booklets. The postmistress, Miss Stewart, and her assistant Marion Kilgour, stand in the doorway. Later the post office and sorting office was at the Logan Street corner in a 1930s building, but that was demolished recently when the office moved into a general store in the new row of shops. (Photograph by kind permission of Douglas Walker)

Main Street, High Blantyre, on a wet day in the 1920s, looking towards Burnbank with the Broompark Road junction halfway down on the left. A horse and cart at the kerb and a small van in the distance complete this atmospheric scene. The site of Smith's garage on the left is now wasteland. The building beyond it remains and the 1898 Co-op store in the right foreground also survives in other hands but nothing else seen here does. Post-war develpoment (or the lack of it) in Main Street has been haphazard and undistinguished – the era has done it no favours. (PPC)

Main Street, nearer Burnbank, with the bank, post office and Andrew Gilmour's shop from left to right. At the far end of the row of shops is Miss Miller's drapery, with the ubiquitous Pullar's of Perth sign visible. The bank is at the corner of Victoria Street. Nothing of this remains. (PPC, published by Brown the stationer)

Looking towards High Blantyre Cross, with the parish church spire in the distance. The local children are out in force to get their pictures taken and they bar the carriageway where Priestfield Road branches off to the left. (PPC, 'Brandon Series', 1903)

117

High Blantyre Cross, c.1915. The Church Hall (left foreground) was replaced because the narrow access to the winding Hunthill Road was making life too difficult for truck drivers seeking a short cut. The Station Cafe (centre) was part of a tenement stretching down Main Street. By the tree is the old water well – now dry. A memorial to those killed in the 1877 Dixon's pit disaster was put up in 1977. (PPC)

The General's Bridge on the old road from High Blantyre to East Kilbride, a fearsome bottleneck in the years before the Expressway was built. The General (Peter) was from nearby Crossbasket House. (PPC, 'Reliable Series' 617, 1905)

Hunthill Road, leading to the West End of Blantyre at Glasgow Road, passed through the hamlet of Barnhill, best known for its inn, the 'Hoolet's Nest' or 'Barnhill Tavern', and is about all that now remains. Two men stand at the inn by a cart in the 1910s and a 1970s view shows it spick and span.

Peth Brae drops down fom Hunthill Road opposite the Barnhill Tavern, a narrow, incredibly steep hill leading down to Millheugh Bridge. Its name derives from 'pech', the Scots word for the breathing pattern caused by such an ascent. The one-legged old gentleman at the foot of the brae here is going to find it even more difficult. The cottages are no more. (PPC, 'Benham Series', 119/43, c. 1910)

The bridge over the Rotten Calder. The road beyond leads past Dechmont Hill towards Cambuslang. The scene looks much the same today, if you ignore today's graffiti and rubbish dumped at the roadside. The arch and parapet have been reconstructed. (PPC, 'Reliable Series', 1903)

Millheugh House stood in its estate to the west of Barnhill. The Millars were here for over 500 years but the house lay deserted by the 1920s and was taken down in the 1950s. (PPC, published by W. Scott, Stationer, High Blantyre)

Auchentibber is about a mile south of the General's Bridge. Led by the local inn-keeper, the exotic Italian Gardens were laid out here by the men from the nearby quarry and mines. The village, its industry and its gardens have gone. (PPC)

Station Road leads from Glasgow Road down to the Clyde, passing the David Livingstone Memorial beyond the railway. Farm Road branches off left where the cart is standing, above, and now leads to a large post-war housing estate. The council houses ('two up & two down' – below) had been recently built and most of the trees taken down. The scene is easily recognisable today. (PPCs: above, c.1932; below, Valentine A6092, 1937, from an image in the St Andrews University Collection)

Mr William Rae consulted as 'Bone Specialist' from Raploch Cottage, No.7, Station Road in Edwardian days. The postcards are captioned 'The Pilgrimage to Blantyre,' and he seems to have had a wide following. What his qualifications and methods were is not known. The youngsters on the right of the group are barefooted. The house looks just the same today. (PPCs, 'Brandon Series', c.1904)

'Blantyre Works Village', completed in 1830. David Dale's first cotton mill was built in 1785 and a dyeworks and weaving factory followed. By the 1860s, 1,800 workers and their families had all the amenities, a school, library, chapel, even a graveyard. The gates closed at 10 p.m. By 1904 all the works were empty and by then the gates had gone. The left gatehouse in the above photograph served as the post office. The low building beyond the other one is still there today. (PPCs: 1905 Victorian photograph; Valentine 41083, 1903)

The Livingstone Memorial, opened on 5 October 1929 by the present Queen Mother, includes the birthplace (left background) and extensive grounds. David Livingstone (1813-1873), a medically qualified missionary of international renown, is Blantyre's most famous son and attempts to detract from his achievements by pointing out any human failings have not diminished his stature. The grounds have been used for everything from Sunday school picnics to events more prestigious if not more important. On this occasion, the Scouts are prominent on the field. (PPC, Valentine, 221197, 1933)

The Old Mill, Blantyre

The Old Mill, by the banks of the Clyde on a postcard posted in 1915. The building had been derelict for twenty years before that date. (PPC, published by William Low, Glasgow)

The original Suspension Bridge, built 1852 and demolished in 1949 by its new owners the National Coal Board. Known as the 'Pey Brig', as much as £10 a week could be collected from the halfpennies of the millworkers. The tollbooths were at the Blantyre end and the old school is at the top of the slope. A new bridge, built in 1952, is itself being replaced. (PPC, Valentine, 213238, 1931)

The Livingstone Memorial Church in Glasgow Road was opened in 1882. Originally the United Presbyterian, it became United Free and in 1929 the established Church of Scotland, through successive re-unions. Livingstone's statue is in a niche in the tower and was unveiled in 1913 by the explorer's daughter. (PPC, published by J.B. White Ltd., A6550, 1930s)

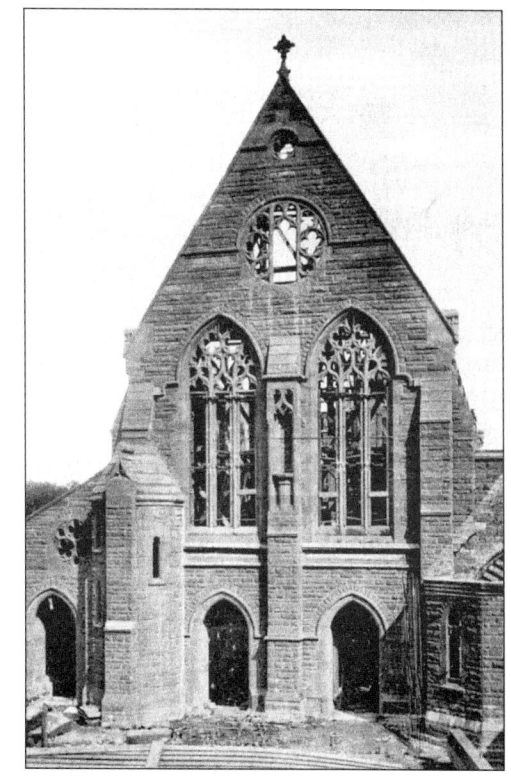

St Joseph's Roman Catholic Church in Mayberry Place was opened in 1905. This early photograph appears to show it under construction, roofless, with building materials in the foreground. In 1877, when the first Catholic priest based in Blantyre since 1567 arrived on the scene, services were being held in houses adapted in Dixon's Rows. (PPC, c.1906)

Spittal Bridge, over the Rotten Calder, on the western edge of Blantyre, was replaced in the 1930s when the tram services ceased and the road was straightened from its original dog-leg route. The overgrown and unsafe old structure remains in place a few yards from the present road. (PPC, c.1908)

Blantyre Priory, founded in the middle of the thirteenth century, was a casualty of the Reformation. Wallace was said to have sheltered here and jumped into the Clyde (some jump!) to escape his pursuers. Another unlikely legend had a tunnel under the Clyde to Bothwell Castle. The last prior was canny enough to become the first Protestant minister of Blantyre. Standing prominently on the banks of the Clyde, the priory's stones were recycled over the centuries and this photograph shows the remains in the early 1920s. No trace remains today. (Photograph by Robert McLeod Snr)